CW00821323

Copyright © GSL Coaching Ltd

If you have received this book from a third party,
please note all rights are reserved by GSL Coaching
Ltd. No part of this publication may be reproduced,
stored in a retrieval system or transmitted in any
form or by any means electronic, mechanical,
photocopying, recording or otherwise, without the
prior written permission of GSL Coaching Ltd.

About the Author

Sarah Tottle is a positive psychologist and coach. She has a special interest in organisational health and well-being, occupational burnout, leadership and development. She has designed and facilitated the Coaching for Change: Positive Psychology in Action workshop, co-authored *Your Pocketful of Inspiration: 100 Ways to Happiness* and is the contributing author for a number of prominent psychology magazines.

Chapter One

What is Coaching?

What is Coaching?

Coaching is a collaborative, goal-orientated relationship that focuses on boosting a client's wellbeing. It uses positive psychological techniques to harness an individual's own personal qualities and resources. In essence, it is a relationship that supports your personal and professional growth.

Coaching is not advice-giving. Rather, it focuses on your own personal qualities, skills and resources, and helps you realise what they are.

Coaching focuses on the individual. It is person-centred, which means the goals you set are personal to you. A coach's role is not to advise, but to help you ascertain your own skills, creativity and awareness so that any decision that is made comes directly from you.

How Can Coaching Motivate Change?

Coaching is about asking yourself questions. It is about focusing on your personal values and what you would like to achieve. It helps you gain deeper self-awareness, that is, it helps you know yourself on a deeper more intimate level. If you know what makes you tick, you know your own triggers. This deeper self-knowledge is the foundations for clarity, focus and assertiveness.

Coaching will show you that you are valuable, that you have resources and skills that can help you achieve goals, and that your goals are important. It will also help you focus on goals that you have actively chosen, rather than being influenced from others.

Coaching will also help you ascertain what your values and beliefs are. This is important, and it comes from greater self-awareness. Once you understand yourself more, you will understand what limiting beliefs or lies have held you back. This is the start of enlightenment.

How Can You Be Your Own Coach?

A professional coach is a great asset and investment, however, not everyone has the time and money to invest in seeing a coach. While I am an advocate of professional coaching, self-development can start in your own home. It can start with you.

The techniques covered in this book will provide you with a unique skillset to coach yourself on a daily basis. You can get proactive in being productive.

The book will provide you with the skills to know yourself better, to feel more at ease with your decisions, to focus on your key strengths and understand your triggers. It will also help you understand what is holding you back, how you have sabotaged yourself in the past, before moving on to focus on your own personal values, brand and style. Finally, it will help you gain a greater sense of vision and purpose for your life, set some key goals to work on and begin a productive and proactive lifestyle moving forward. Happy Coaching!

What is self-awareness?

Self-awareness is simple. It simply means knowing yourself more. When you understand yourself better, you know what makes you tick, what your triggers are (what provokes you), and what makes you feel your best.

Self-awareness is a key foundation to start coaching yourself. It is an exploration of self. It is taking time out to answer the questions you have about life- or any existential queries you may possess. If you don't have questions, don't worry. Generating self-awareness is as much about giving yourself time to gain clarity. It can be scary to take time out from the busyness of life and have a good think. However, in doing so you can avoid any potential crises further down the line.

We never really take time out to sit alone with our thoughts, to question our actions, our assumptions and beliefs about life. But, this is key to gaining self-awareness. You may be thinking where is the time? However, time is an investment you need to make. That odd five minutes alone, or a solitary lunch hour can help gain a sense of clarity and greater vision. You could even make a daily or weekly change to your schedule, for instance, getting up one hour earlier to focus on your thoughts and learn more about you.

Key Rules to Building Self-Awareness

1) Take time out to explore your thoughts. Write down a list of

questions you have been pondering, but never really had time to answer. Let your mind flow and question what comes to mind, write it down.

2) Take time out to do nothing. How do you feel? Note what emotions come up. What are these emotions? Write them down. What could these emotions be telling you? For instance, do you feel restless or bored? Are you completely relaxed or do you feel deadbeat?

3) Journal. Begin to journal how you feel. Write down your thoughts on a daily basis and reflect back. Write about what gave you joy and what made you angry, defensive,

frustrated or sad. These insights can be incredibly useful in furthering your self-awareness.

4) Seek feedback. Ask trusted sources to provide you with feedback on how they see you in your role. You can ask a trusted family member, colleague or friend. Ask them to be polite, but honest. This feedback loop will bring in greater awareness of your 'blind-spots', the areas of yourself that exist, but you lack awareness.

Strength Building

Building upon your strengths is the direct result of self-awareness. We cannot know our strengths and values without first knowing ourselves. Our strengths are what we are good at. They are what we enjoy. They give us the ability to stay in the zone, or what psychologists call 'the flow', where we perform optimally, taking our limiting beliefs out of the picture.

It is better to become a master of our strengths, but first we must know what they are. To do this, write down a list of your talents, achievements are enjoyments. If you struggle to find your strengths, ask a trusted friend to help you identify them.

Once you have a list of your strengths, keep
a visible record. Focus on your
achievements to date and this will increase
motivation for achievement in the future.
As a coach, I prefer to have visible
reminders of my strengths and that which I
am talented at. It helps navigate those
moments of self-doubt that creep up on us
all. I am armed with a reminder of my
achievements that I can strike those
niggling doubts down with.

Success
x x

Success is as much about being aware of
your strengths, and building upon your
existing skill-set, as it is learning
something new. Really explore what your
strengths mean to you. If your friend

describes you as passionate, find a more suitable and authentic way of expressing this that resonates with you.

Finally, our strengths may overlap with colleagues and friends, but they are also the little nuances within our personality- perhaps the way we think or do things in a particular way that is unique to us.

Your inner child

If we have been in a rut for a long time, devoid of any form of creative expression, we can almost forget what it is like to feel, to have passion, to be us. The feeling of being trapped or stuck is common and it often strikes when we have fallen off the road less travelled, or at least the road we are meant to be walking along. If you are still struggling to understand your strengths, and have forgotten who you truly are, reverting back to childhood memories can often help.

Children often have a freedom that allows them to creatively express and enjoy life, devoid of the psychological prisons and restrictions adults place upon themselves. By reverting back to childhood memories, we can gain a deeper understanding of what we enjoy. Ask your inner child what they love to do? What are they passionate about? What fun memories did you have as a child? What were you doing? Where were you? And with whom did you enjoy that time? Those questions can pave way for insight into what you truly love to do and are a great way of understanding your strengths.

Triggers: Psychological Triggers and How You Can Resolve Them

A trigger is something that sets off a psychological memory. It is something that is very personal that can cause you to have a flashback of something that happened many years before. However, while some triggers are conscious, many of our triggers are unconscious, or at least beyond conscious awareness. They can be a hindrance to personal growth and understanding them through self-awareness can help us move forward and handle situations in a calmer manner.

While our triggers may be activated through the senses, for instance, seeing someone that visibly looks like a relative that has upset us, often a trigger is activated through an attitude. As a child, you may have felt unheard. If in adulthood you meet someone that dismisses something you say, this may result in an unnatural reaction based on an unconscious trigger.

We can be more aware of our triggers through being conscious of our behaviour. What makes us happy? What makes us sad? Is there any repetition in a behaviour and is it expressed with multiple people? If so, this could be an unresolved trigger that needs to be worked through.

The first thing to overcome a trigger is to take a step back during heightened emotionality. Recognise that the act of emotionality is a reactive response, not a rational one. Once recognition has taken place, choose to step back and ask what caused the distress, anger or other negative emotion. Once you are in a neutral emotional state, you can begin to see what behaviours, situations or physicality triggers negative emotions in you. It could be as simple as realising that you are feeling over worked and have not eaten properly in a few days. You feel more vulnerable at this time, and therefore, it is better to respond at a different moment in time.

Take time to understand your triggers, and while self-coaching is a valuable tool, if your triggers are getting in the way to the extent you need additional support, work through them with an accredited coach or therapist.

Chapter Two

Barriers to Success

Barriers to success come in a number of ways. This chapter will look at the different ways we get in the way of ourselves, we make it difficult to progress, and we often hold ourselves back. The chapter will look at concepts such as self-sabotage, impostor syndrome, self-confidence and esteem, lack of vision and clarity and limiting beliefs.

Self-sabotage

Self-sabotaging is an enemy within. We need to overcome self-sabotaging behaviours so we can grow and be prepared to accept the good things life has to offer. Sabotaging ourselves can be both conscious and unconscious, and often equates to not feeling good enough to enjoy the opportunities that arise. We limit ourselves based on our flawed sense of being, our lack of values and the beliefs we hold about ourselves.

Often self-sabotaging behaviours arise through childhood, and in that sense, they need to be worked through. We can be heroes, only when we work through the demons in our minds. We can cast down those demons, and live a life based on authenticity and truth. Self-sabotage can be unconscious, and only through thorough analysis can it be dealt with. As a child, you may have been told you were no good at reading out loud. This belief, based on a one off ill-informed comment from a parent or teacher, has led to the ongoing belief that you are not competent, or have an inability to read confidently. This long held belief, almost under conscious awareness, impacts on daily work functions as it becomes almost impossible for the adult self to hold a meeting which involves reading out loud from slides. Working through the issue, both on a conscious basis, as the adult self, is useful in seeing the belief for what it is. It is no longer viable.

Self-sabotage causes us to hold back from what is rightfully ours. It can impact on the

choice of work we do, from under-
achieving to not choosing the correct
profession, to also choosing mediocrity in
relationships. We do not see ourselves as
being of worth, of value, and act out,
through sabotaging behaviours, to prevent
us moving forward. We choose behaviours
we know will sabotage the results we are
aiming for, creating a self-fulfilling
prophecy, feeding into the image that we
deserve less.

To stop self-sabotage, we must see it for
what it is. We are held accountable for our
own bahaviours, and here-forth, we must
take a thorough examination of ourselves.
Only when we become more self-aware,

when we objectively look at our behaviours, when we bring the unconscious to conscious awareness, can we prevent the very cycle that hinders us.

Impostor Syndrome

Do you ever feel like a fraud? That you got to where you were by chance? Through a fluke, perhaps? That one day you will be found out and that you are just one step from the biggest mistake ever? If so, these thoughts are the thoughts of an impostor syndrome sufferer. Impostor Syndrome was coined by two American Clinical Psychologists in the 1970s as a definition for high achieving individuals that are unable to feel like they achieved their goals through their own capabilities, but rather fear being exposed as a phony.

Impostor syndrome is highly prevalent among high achieving professionals, and although more women than men feel it, it can affect both male and females alike. It is something to evaluate from an objective perspective, knowing its prevalence, reflection on achievements is key. The first stage is to understand that impostor syndrome is real and prevalent. This alone can help offset any thoughts of being a fraud. Understanding that many people that have achieved much in life also feel this way, can be beneficial to working through feelings of imposter syndrome. Having that knowledge, coupled with an objective look at your own achievements can be helpful. For instance, you may want to look at your achievement and how you got there. Did you do anything that was particularly praised? Can you ask for honest feedback from a supervisor about your talents? Did you work hard and therefore deserve what you got? What would being really honest feel like? It is often when we are truly vulnerable, that we are truly confident. Exposing our thoughts as failures may help thwart them, because we have people that can encourage us with the truth of our capabilities.

Choose a trusted mentor at work to help alleviate your concerns. If this feels too much, write it down. Then talk to those answers as if you were talking to a colleague or friend.

Increasing Confidence and Self-Esteem

You are a work in progress and confidence is something we must build like a muscle. There are a number of ways to increase confidence and self-esteem. One of which is daily affirmations. Choose to reflect on your achievements, characteristics that people love about you and your positive qualities each day. You can write a list to carry with you. If this is too challenging, ask a trusted friend to write a few things that they love about you.

Make daily changes to your life. What are some of the big and small things you would love to do? What would you like to wear? Be bold, try a new lipstick or nail colour, compliment yourself, encourage and uplift others. Choose to be brave and take some leaps, telling yourself it is important for the growth of your esteem. It is important to congratulate yourself too. Begin to celebrate the big and the small.

You can also keep a gratitude journal. Choose to write down the five things you are grateful for. It could be as small as the food you had for breakfast. Journaling has proven scientific benefits for the brain. Not only does it help rewire it so you begin to feel incrementally more positive, but it helps get your thoughts out of your head. You can see the things you are happy with and you can reflect on them daily, weekly and monthly. Try it! You may well be surprised.

Seeking Clarity and Moving Beyond a Limited Vision

Without vision, we run round in circles. It is important to set realistic and achievable goals. Not only does constant goal setting keep us motivated, but it also gives us something to look forward to. A vision gives us structure- we know where we are heading. While the next chapter focuses on how we can develop goals and our vision, this section looks at why we may not set them.

Often it is indecisiveness that stops us from setting goals. If this is the case, it is often wise to note that taking some action is better than none. At least then we are heading somewhere! We can always backtrack if it turns out to be the wrong road, and we can even use and harness the skills we learnt from that journey in a positive way.

Becoming more decisive is key. To do so, it is recommended that you keep a list of all the things you enjoy doing and also the things you are good at. When choosing a career or a course of study, you can refer to that list to help you decide.

Seeking clarity is important, and while it may be difficult to achieve in our frantic paced way of life, it is not impossible. Take time out from the chaos of life, tune into nature, harness your creative juices, but above all else, listen to that small voice. A walk in nature is one of the best ways to gain insight and deeper clarity. If that is not possible, find your quiet space. This can be a room without distraction. Take a blank piece of paper and explore whatever comes to mind.

When I need more clarity, I venture out in nature, coffee in hand, taking my journal to explore any new ideas that come to me. I also use brainstorming sessions to capture ideas, writing any key thoughts that come to mind. Once one or two ideas come, I am able to draw from them and add more, creating a bigger vision and picture of what I would like to achieve.

So often, it is the *why* behind the *what* that we need to ask. What is the purpose and why do I want to achieve this? The *why* factor is what keeps us motivated to achieve, even when there is an obstacle in the way of the *what*.

Limiting Beliefs

Limiting beliefs are the beliefs that hold us back. Often again, they are both usually unconscious, as well as that which others have prescribed us. Limiting beliefs are any beliefs we hold about ourselves that hold us back. We discredit our achievements or even our personal mission in life, because of the fears that we tell ourselves. Limiting beliefs can sometimes disguise themselves as positive ideologies, but if they are not authentic, then they are sabotaging us from achieving what we truly want. We imprison ourselves with the fears and lies that consume us, and therefore any limiting beliefs need to be challenged and thwarted, paving way for authentic living, achieving our goals with much more ease.

While some limiting beliefs are obvious, such as the words we often speak over ourselves, others are less overt. Other limiting beliefs, disguised as positive assumptions, can equally hinder our growth. If we tell ourselves we are being selfless, constantly helping others is our nature, but not expecting anything in return, this can also be a recipe for disaster.

Lack of assertiveness can hinder growth, because while we may put the livelihood of others before us, and such a pursuit is honourable, if we constantly sacrifice our own needs this may hinder our own authentic growth. If you hold back on what you are truly capable of, but wear your self-sacrifice as a badge of honour, it is not only you that fails. Your compromise withholds your talents from many others.

More obvious limiting beliefs include feeling lazy, feeling like a failure, worrying that you will not succeed and believing you are not worthy of anything good. Take an objective stance against your limiting beliefs. Take time out to challenge them with more realistic thinking. Understanding where they came from can be helpful, and then utilise other empowering beliefs in their place.

Empowering beliefs focus on the here and now, and the future. They encourage you to realise that your past does not equate your future. Whatever mistakes or failures you deem to have had in the past does not make you. Rather, focus your own thoughts on what you have learned along the way. Mirror other successful people. What does their life tell you? Often their own adversities and perceived failures can be a source of comfort.

Coach's Top Tips:

In order for you to gain greater self-
awareness and an understanding of your
thoughts, keep a thought journal for a
couple of weeks to capture your beliefs.
This will show up any negative beliefs.
Focus on what you thought, and write
down the context or situation that led to
the thought. Is there any evidence to
support this belief? Once you have a list of
beliefs and negative thoughts, you can
challenge them with your list of positive
qualities and affirmations.

Use the Downward Arrow Technique, a
technique to uncover core or limiting
beliefs, to help you discover more. Firstly,

focus on the thought that is bothering you. What is that thought? Secondly, ask yourself what it means about you? There may be a few answers. Keep this going until you get to the underlying problem- this is your core belief. Of course, beliefs can be positive, and we must keep them, but when they hinder us, it is useful to uncover them and challenge them too. Core beliefs are often linked to core fears. Core fears are often extremely irrational, and uncovering them can be useful to challenging that fear too. Follow the same process of discovery to uncover your irrational core fears.

You can also use techniques like Thought Stopping, saying *STOP!* when a negative thought comes to mind. This will prevent possible catastrophising, escalating the problem without evidence. You can change what you are thinking instead.

Chapter Three

Dreams and Goals

Defining Your Own Personal Success

Success is subjective. It is subjective because it is uniquely defined. One cannot be successful, if their own definition has not first been coined by one's authentic self. Success is only success if it belongs to the individual.

This is why we must continue to strive for our own personal definition of success. We must first define what success means to us. This has nothing to do with what others are doing, their own personal definition of success, or even socially prescribed definitions. It has to do with the life you want to live. It has to do with boldness, stepping out from the norm, and challenging the status quo. Most people living society's definition of success are no longer happy. Their joy has been zapped as they trudge through a rat race that was never paved to help a person's growth. Do you really want to be living that type of life? Step away. Define your own goals, value system and beliefs. Let those govern your choices.

It may be that your definition of success means freedom, working less, and perhaps even having less in the way of material goods. It could be that the corporate career is for you, that you do love city life, and you want to shop until you drop. Whatever definition of success you have, it is important that that definition actually belongs to you. Socially prescribed norms only hinder our authenticity and ultimately hold us back. So whatever you do, define your own version of success, a success that is authentically you.

Your Unique Brand

How do you see yourself? Is what you show the world congruent with what is on the inside? Do you voice your values and opinions so people get to know the real you? Or do you hold yourself back? Are you worried about what people may think if they knew you better? All these fears can hold us back. They withhold our unique selling point (USP) and that is ultimately what we have to offer the world. If we hold back, if our outside and inside are not congruent, we are the ones that lose out. We cannot have authentic relationships, attract the right people, and explore the right opportunities, if what we are projecting to the world does not readily align with who we are.

Your unique brand is you. It is the real version of you. What is your USP? What idiosyncrasies, quirks and traits do you possess, that could be of value to others? If you are not being real at this current moment, begin to ask yourself why you are holding back. If it is out of fear, ask yourself what the long-term consequence would be to remain in that state. If you fear that you would no longer be accepted by peers, would this peer group really be right for you?

Finally, you can make daily choices in your quest for authenticity. You can begin to map out the life that you want to project. Choose clothes that reflect who you are. Remember you are your own personal brand. Begin to explore what that means to you.

Coach's Top Tips:

Find someone you admire and find
inspirational to mirror. You can model the
way they do things, or follow their success
strategy. This is particularly useful for
career success. How did your role model
get to where they are? If you do not have
the opportunity to shadow them, be brave
and ask them. What did your role model
do? Ask for advice? Imitate their success.
Check your progress and then develop your
own path.

Chapter Four

Developing Your Vision

Understanding Your Motives

It is important to assess your motives for doing something. This is imperative to achieving your goals, and ultimately your vision. If your motives don't belong to you, i.e. they are inherited from your parents, or are socially prescribed, then you will be less likely to achieve them.

What are your personal beliefs? Do your beliefs come from you? Why do you believe the things you do? Questions like this help to assess the validity of your goals and values, because they allow you to check in with yourself and see whether the belief system you have is actually yours to begin with.

I am a firm believer in challenging the status quo, the current mode of doing things, and cultural norms. In some sense, I see myself as counter-cultural, but even these beliefs need to be challenged. We do not need years of psychotherapy to breed this awareness, a daily dose of reflective journaling can also help the process, but exploratory questions are essential.

Moving From Motives to Action

Every action we take has a preceding motive. We are motivated into action because of our values. It is our motives that lead us.

If our motives are predefined for us, if they are the result of external expectations, then we must make a thorough analysis of them. We can assess whether our rationale is authentic. Because almost all action is the result of motivation- be this the life choices we make on relationships, career, family- and as a result challenging motives can shift things so that you begin to take a more authentic approach to living. In this sense, we must assess our motives wisely. Inauthentic motives will compromise your sense of fulfilment. Unchallenged beliefs can lead to an inauthentic life.

Choosing an action that directly aligns with your authentic self can make all the

difference in life. To do so, it is
recommended you follow these steps:
firstly, begin to question your belief system.
Ask yourself why you believe what you do.
Are your values your own? Or have they
resulted from the beliefs of others? Do you
follow in the footsteps of your role models
because you really want to, or do you feel a
sense of expectation to do so? Such an
analysis can be very helpful in progressing
towards your own authentic life vision.

Remember, if your motives for achievement
are externally prescribed, you may be less
likely to achieve them. If your motives are
about receiving external gratification and
approval, you will almost always resent the
life you lead.

Visualisation

Visualisation is key to achieving your goals and creating success. Movie stars, sports champions and other successful leaders use the art of visualisation to achieve success in the minor and the major. Visualisation, as a tool, can be used for as little as seeing or imagining success in a meeting or interview, to as big as imagining your life achievements in one sitting.

I often use creative visualisation to help succeed at work. I imagine what I will wear to a meeting, how I will feel and the answers that I will have to questions that may arise. I use imagination and visualisation to feel the success prior to attaining it. It helps me to feel more confident. As the mind cannot differentiate between imagination and reality, visualising success before attaining it in reality really helps to achieve goals. It can give a sense of calmness, lowering blood pressure in high anxiety situations, and allows the autonomic nervous system to function optimally.

In order to visualise, it is important to get comfortable, removing any distractions from your life, and go into a space or room where no one will disturb you. You can even play some relaxing music in the background; low enough that it does not overload your senses, but high enough to hear its effects. Then begin to count down from ten to zero, with each interval telling yourself you are becoming more and more relaxed. Start saying the following: 'my mind is clear, I am relaxed. I can think and imagine with ease'. Once you get to zero, feeling the relaxed state from head to toes, allow your mind to dream and explore. Feel yourself being confident and at ease, relaxed and ready. Begin to think of a situation that you want to succeed in, and then explore within your imagination, the feeling of success. See yourself as confident, imagine what you will do and say in the situation. Describe and imagine what you are wearing, how confident you feel, and how well you articulate yourself. Once you feel relaxed and confident, assured of your success, begin the count back up from zero to ten. With each interval, begin to tell yourself you are relaxed, feeling positive, good in every way, you feel at ease and are now ready to succeed. You have now succeeded in the art of visualisation.

The next step in visualisation is to develop your life vision. Having something to look forward to not only gives you structure in life, but is also linked to higher levels of mental wellbeing. The structure provides a plan to keep you on course, meaning your life feels like it has greater purpose. Your daily and weekly goals also have more meaning, because they are placed as part of a bigger life plan.

In order to define a vision, you can also use the previous visualisation technique where you use your imagination and explore what your perfect life would look like. You can use your imagination to describe the type of work you would be doing, the clothes you will be wearing, where you would be living and who you would be spending time with. You can use the techniques to focus on four key areas: home life, location, relationships, finances and career, but you are not limited to just these areas. It is a guide to get you started.

Once you get used to frequent visualisation, you can then add to these ideas. It is advisable to write your thoughts down. It is also recommended you stay focused on a five year or ten year plan, which means the results feel more tangible and attainable. Keep your plan safe and refer to this on an ongoing basis.

Your five year plan

Having developed your vision and subsequently written it down, it is time to explore how you can achieve this. Your overall vision is your grand plan, but you need steps to achieve this too.

The first step is a step often purported in Neuro-Linguistic Programming. It is focused on chunking down. You see your plan, but you write a list of steps needed to attain the full plan through breaking them down into smaller goals. Each goal must then be broken down further into more manageable yearly targets and from then on, monthly, weekly and daily targets.

A to-do list is helpful to keep track of the weekly goals. It provides structure and writing a list has proven benefits. You are much more likely to achieve your goals if you write them down.

It is important to ask key questions regarding your plan. What must I do this month to achieve my plan? What must I work on this week to achieve my goals this month? Do this process until you have broken down to smaller daily goals. Remember, the smaller daily steps help us achieve the bigger life goals. The bigger life plans also feel much more attainable when we have chunked them down into manageable bites. Be like the ants, they start small.

Coach's Top Tips:

Use the visualisation strategy to visualise new beliefs. Choose a belief you would rather have over a belief that is hindering you. Visualise the belief you want. Describe what you see, hear and feel. Imagine believing this new belief. Repeat until the belief is a part of your new belief system.

Chapter five

Planning Your Goals

According to Carl Sandberg, 'nothing happens unless first a dream'. Our goals and visions are first dreamed in our mind, whether they are what we wear or eat that day, or even as grand as the vision we have for our life. Seeing the image starts the process to planning.

There are some essentials to help you plan your goals. A number of useful models have been proven to boost motivation and dedication to achieving our goals. These include the SMART model and the T-Grow.

The SMART model stands for *Specific, Measurable, Achievable, Realistic* and *Time-Bound*. It is important that your goals are expressed in a positive manner, that they are realistic and attainable in the sense that you could achieve them with motivation and tenacity, and that you are specific. Your goals can be worked on straight away. You can begin to develop smaller goals that align with your bigger and grander plans.

The time has come to set a SMART goal or two. Keep your goals to a minimum to begin with. Focusing on up to three is a better strategy, especially in the early days of goal setting. If goal setting is new to you, it is a good idea to start small, building your confidence along the way.

Having used the strategy in the *Developing Your Vision* chapter, using the SMART acronym, write down a specific goal following these steps. Remember, having been through the brainstorming process, it is important to add a strategy to achieving your goal too. This could be done through exploring all the options you have and mapping out a process and time-line to do this. SMART can also help assess the validity of your goal as you begin to ask questions on whether the goal is realistic and you can meet it within a given time-frame.

Making sure your goal is **specific** is the first point. You must be clear on what you would like to achieve. Your goal must also be **measurable**. You must be able to measure any improvements you have made towards the goal, as well as know when you have successfully achieved it. In essence, you can see the fruition of your goal. Your goal must also be **achievable**, in the sense, that it can be attained. The achievement of smaller goals will help increase confidence and motivation to achieve other goals too. Similarly, your goal must be **realistic**. While your goal should be challenging, you must set goals that are realistic and relevant to you. They must also be goals that have been set by you, rather than other people. In this sense, they must come from the heart. Lastly, a goal must be **time-bound**. You must clearly set

a time-limit for achieving your goals. Be specific on the time-frame for achieving your SMART goals. Your goal may be to run a ten kilometre run. Your time-frame may be three months' time. You can start to use your SMART goal to assess a strategy to achieve this aim, by planning how much you need to run each day or week to attain your goal.

The T-GROW model

Similar to the SMART model, T-GROW allows you to set realistic and attainable goals, providing a space to define a strategy to achieve them.

T-GROW stands for *Topic, Goal, Reality, Options* and *Way Forward*. It is useful as it takes into context your current situation.

You can develop goals through the T-GROW model by exploring what you would like to achieve. You may not be so specific at this stage, so using the brainstorming exercises in the last chapter, start to explore the topic at hand. What is it that you would like to work towards? Begin to think about the larger topic, and chunk it down into manageable bites. These smaller bites are your new goals.

You can then use the goals explored within the topic and list a few of them you would like to achieve. Ask yourself which goal is most important and why? Have there been any obstacles to achieving your goals in the past? What were these? Are they there now and can they be overcome? What must you do to overcome them? If this is a goal you have had for a while, why is now the time to achieve it? Why not before? What is different about this time? How will you celebrate when you achieve this goal? It is important to paint a clear picture of your situation and then focus on what you would like to achieve in the here and now.

Having found a couple of primary goals to work on, begin to look at your current reality. What is your current situation? Can you think of any obstacles that may get in the way of achieving these goals? If so, what are the options to overcome them? What could you do to change your situation so it is more favourable to achieving your goal? Begin to think outside the box, finding solutions to any potential issues that may arise.

The next stage is to focus on options. These are the opportunities you have to make your goals more attainable. You can begin exploring who and what may be of help to you. What options do you have? It is important that you explore the options through brainstorming. The use of visualisation and relaxation can help open the unconscious part of the mind, which is helpful in providing creative input.

Finally, the Way-Forward allows you to think about the multiple choices you have and begin to form a strategy to achieving the goals you have in mind. In this case, draw up your plan of action, being specific on the goals you would like to achieve and making steps to achieve them. Look at the options you have for attaining your goals, and utilise them within your strategy. You may, for instance, need to take an hour's break from the family home and need to ask for assistance from other members of your family. Or you may need to sign up to do additional courses for learning. It is important at this stage to utilise the resourcefulness you have gathered through brainstorming your options.

Setting Aims and Objectives

I am a firm believer in setting aims and objectives. In fact, every New Year, I set a list of aims for the year. They help set the year off in positive motion, and give me some structure for the year. It also allows me to have things to look forward to, giving me a sense of accomplishment when I have achieved my goals.

Similarly, I also set a list of objectives for achieving my goals. It may be that I want more freedom, or I want to be more altruistic, and having my maxims for life or objectives clear gives me the all-important *why* to my *what*.

I am also an avid believer in having my own personal mission statement. The mission statement combines all my life objectives. It also includes what type of legacy I would like to leave behind. How would you like others to remember you when you are gone? Or what would you like people to say at your 80th birthday? What words would

you want people to describe you by? Such a
mission statement can enhance our
purpose in life, adding true authenticity to
our living. If today was your last day on
earth, how would you choose to live it?
Choose to add these principles into your
daily living, knowing that regrets and fears
only hold us back.

Showing Commitment

Commitment to one's goals is largely due to
that all important *why* factor. Commitment
is a form of tenacity and dedication that
can only really be achieved when we have
true authentic belief in our goals. Our

purpose and our goals must come from within, not family or friends.

Commitment is a socially desirable trait that reinforces our belief in ourselves and the belief that others have within us. It is therefore important to manifest commitment in our work. It is easier to commit and be dedicated to something that aligns with our purpose, or something greater than ourselves. That is why altruistic tendencies bring about greater rewards. The altruistic person is contributing to something far greater than themselves.

Motivation- How to develop it?

Motivation is like a muscle. We must harness its use to build it. It grows stronger through constant usage. We become more motivated through personal productivity and accomplishment.

There are a number of tips to developing motivation:

- Set attainable goals
- Achieve these goals
- Focus on what you can do
- Use affirmations and focus on past achievements
- Reward your achievements

Developing Habits

Changing your habits also entails commitment and dedication. In order to develop a new habit, or change an existing one, you must want to do so. You must also believe that it is possible and that you have the power within to do so.

Habits can be changed in as little as a couple of months. The process of changing habit starts with ongoing affirmations. This process includes affirming the belief of what you want, and making incremental and daily changes too. Changing a habit may be challenging and difficult at first. This is to be expected if one of your habits has taken years to be ingrained. Overnight success is not to be expected, but the expectation of change is necessary.

There are two ways to change a habit. One may result in going cold turkey, but relies on a deprivation model, and rarely lasts. This is often used in yo-yo dieting, with a vicious cycle of negative feelings and self-loathing when the new habit has not been formed. The alternative is to make changes in increments, and has a much higher success rate. This is especially so when coupled with ongoing use of affirmations. For instance, you may want to develop healthy eating habits. It is first necessary to be specific on what eating healthy means to *you*. You can then plan to make small and ongoing changes, until the majority of your week is filled with lean and clean meals. In this case, it is important to make a plan, starting small to begin with, and making ongoing changes every day or week to your meals. At the same time, you can add daily affirmations, repeating that 'I eat healthy. I eat food that provides health and wellbeing to my body. I make healthy choices.' Use your affirmations regularly throughout the day- it is recommended that seven times is the minimum, ingraining those new thoughts into your mind.

You can choose your own new habits, applying the same principles and developing your own personal affirmations to live by. Celebrate your victories too.

Remember, when developing your affirmations, stay focused on the present moment, using the phrase 'I am' rather than 'I will'. Habits may take time to change, but you can do it.

Reframing Failure

Our good intentions may fail us from time to time and that is ok. Failing is part of doing. It is important not to be so hard on yourself. Many great people have failed before achieving their greatness. If you fail at something, begin to get into the process of learning from it, rather than focusing on feeling like a failure. At those moments, give yourself some compassion, and choose to move forward taking on board what you have learned in the process.

Failure can be a positive that we learn from. It can also prevent us from going further down the wrong path. We can learn to celebrate failure as much as success when we know we have learnt something valuable from it.

If you have failed at a goal or changing a habit, know that you are human. It can happen to anyone and indeed it has. Remember that failure is not the end of your achievement and that you can still pick yourself up again and work towards changing that habit or goal. Ask yourself what have you learned from this failure?

What can you do differently next time? Am I actually on the right path? Or perhaps should I change my goals? Reframing failure as a positive will help you achieve victory in the long run.

Coach's Top Tips:

Follow the OSCAR model. This stands for *outcome, situation, choices, actions* and *review.* What is the outcome you require? What is your current situation? What is happening now? Be clear on the context and situation. What choices do you have? What have you done so far? What worked? What did not? How can you build on this? What can you do now? What actions will you take? And how will you review this progress?

Do a cost benefit analysis. What are the costs and benefits of achieving your goal? What potential opportunities and obstacles will you have? How can you build

on your strengths and overcome any
challenges?

Taking action is the first step to success.
What can you do differently to what you
have done so far? Then make a plan.

Chapter Six

Solution-Focused Self-Coaching

Time-management

Time management is key to establishing
and setting goals. It is good practice to
getting into managing your time more
effectively. Time is lost when it is ill-used.
It is also lost through over-commitment
and lack of assertion of your wants and
needs. Time is finite for the purpose of
achieving your goals. We lose time through
committing to plans that are not part of
our purpose, or helping people achieve
their dreams, but sacrificing our own
desires. It is all well, and recommended to
support others in building their dreams,
but support only comes from an alignment
with their vision too. If you work for a large
corporation, but your plan in life is to sell

organic health food, then you are wasting your precious resources on someone else's vision.

Being able to say *no* is key to effective time management. Begin the process of only saying *yes* to that which you desire to do. No explanation is necessary. I give you full authority to saying *yes* to your life desires, and *no* to the things that you do not wish to do (within reason). Stop letting people put onto you. Stop allowing them to take advantage and begin to take full ownership of your own dreams and desires.

Time management also warrants careful planning. It utilises your own personal resources and energy cycle. If you know you are more productive and filled with energy in the morning, but slump mid-afternoon, start planning your schedule around your energy cycles. Also, take note of when your energy hits its slump. What can this possibly tell you about yourself? Is this a natural part of your circadian rhythm or perhaps do you need to eat more or consume more water too?

There are a number of resources to use to manage time, but strategies such as energy management and sleep hygiene are all linked. You cannot expect to manage your time wisely and achieve more, if you sleep too little. Your levels of productivity are a direct result of your energy levels, and these are influenced by food and sleep patterns. Eat regularly, rest more, drink more water and choose to sleep enough hours to suit your body cycle.

Begin each week with your weekly expectations. Start by placing your tasks into what is important and urgent and work through these tasks at the beginning of the week. Get the worst tasks out of the way first, knowing that whatever follows, will be easier and more manageable. Those tasks that are not urgent and not important can be left until the end of the week when energy levels are usually faltering.

I also choose to use a To-Do list. While some people disagree with its use, it helps me have clarity on what I need to do and also get my thoughts out of my head and onto paper. This gives me that important clarity to get ahead. At the end of each day, reflect on your achievements, and write a list of goals to achieve the following day.

Scheduling time wisely is also important. Making sure that adequate time has been given to prepare for and run meetings is necessary. If travel is necessary, schedule enough time into the diary for travel time and any possible interruptions. This will ensure that you arrive at destinations with ease, and feel relaxed, preserving valuable energy for the important stuff.

Productivity 101

Are you making time for the important stuff? Do you constantly feel like you are running on an empty tank? If so, your productivity may be faltering and you may need an energy re-haul.

The following tips will increase productivity:

- Take time out when needed
- Rest more
- Celebrate your successes
- Watch your sleep patterns
- Drink more water
- Avoid work distractions
- Take a break every 50 minutes
- Eat regularly and healthily
- Take your annual leave

- Stop working over-time
- Work smart, not hard. Challenge your thinking that more hours means more work
- Take a walk at lunch time
- Get more fresh air
- Enjoy nature
- Remember to switch off from social media
- Turn off the news
- Do not watch TV or check your phone two hours before bed

Making changes to your lifestyle based on the above tips will help boost productivity levels, but it is also important to assess whether you are where you want to be too. If you are in the wrong job, or committing to the wrong goal, this can also impact on your energy levels. Deflation is a sign that you are not doing what you should be. Listen to your levels of motivation. If you become energised and passionate about one goal, but not another, it is time to refocus your energy on what really matters.

Passion and energy are important enablers of success. What fires your soul is clue to what you should be doing in life. You will master the art of productivity when there is passion in your tummy!

Positive Self-Talk

There is power in language. It can make or break a person's success. Many words have been used and internalised in childhood and have impacted on people even into adulthood.

The use of positive affirmations is one way to reframe your thinking. The use of positive self-talk is useful in ingraining a positive outlook in your mind. Become aware of your self-talk. Is it purposeful? Would you say the same things to your best friend? Would you still be beautiful if the words you spoke to yourself were written all over your body for all to see? How useful is this negative language and where did it come from? Are you still harbouring fears from that which were spoken over you as a child? If so, it is time to move on. It is time to use affirmations to help challenge your beliefs.

Keep a list of all your positive qualities and refer to them daily, or even as often as you need. Begin to affirm what you would like to achieve on a regular basis, reframing your doubts and fears each time. You may want to challenge any can't do attitudes with a realistic response. Fear is a powerful weapon that keeps us in our comfort zone, but it is often based on misguided assumptions. Challenging your fears with realistic thinking is useful. This can be done through the avoidance of generalisations- the "I always fail" approach- and thwarting this belief through finding times when you have been successful.

We must always try and avoid fortune telling and catastrophising our situations. This means seeing problems that do not actually exist, or foreseeing a disaster when there is no evidence of impending doom. Doing so only feeds into our fears, further holding us back.

Stay focused on your use of daily positive affirmations. You can write your affirmations down, but I also recommend the use of a gratitude diary. This is a helpful way of journaling all that you are thankful for. It has a powerful impact on the mind,

making ongoing changes that will make
you feel more optimistic overall.

My own personal recommendation is to
write a list of affirmations that I have as life
maxims. These include: "I am kind. I am
generous. I show grace to all people." It
feeds into my higher purpose in life, but is a
reminder of the positive qualities I possess
or wish to develop. It is what I stand for in
life.

Positive Psychology

One of the major advancements in psychological knowledge is through the work of prominent psychologist, Martin Seligman, on the science of happiness. It challenged mainstream psychology's approach that focused on the pathological. Seligman posited a theory of happiness, with objectives for achieving wellbeing. Part of the positive psychology movement focuses on the need for relationships, for altruistic deeds through random acts of kindness, to living an authentic life and serving a greater purpose.

Positive psychology has been fundamental to my own life, both as a practitioner and a person. I have used the concepts in positive psychology to embrace authentic living, challenging the status quo, and harnessing my own unique skillset and potential. By being more authentic, choosing lifestyle choices that align with my own value system, I have been able to work on my goals, utilising my own creative potential.

The key points in positive psychology focus on daily doses of gratitude, cultivating a mind-set of thankfulness, through the use of a gratitude journal. I recommend you add five new things you are thankful for each day.

The second point is harnessing creativity. Creativity is cultivated through taking time out from the chaos and being in a positive environment. You will know what environment works for you. My own personal creativity is harnessed through being in a room that is minimalist, with the least amount of distractions. You may need a room filled with ideas, colours and inspiration. Do whatever works for you. The focus is on the positive nature of the environment. It is important to use affirmations, as negativity can hinder creativity.

Once you have utilised your creative potential, you will begin to see that you are more focused. Creativity allows you to get into the 'flow'; this is a state of being that psychologists describe as being completely focused, devoid of knowledge of time and distraction. You will become completely enthralled in the moment, not thinking about the past or the future. Your creative juices will be flowing and you will feel at ease.

Neuroplasticity

The brain has an ability to reorganise itself; to change its neural pathways and to develop new ingrained ways of thinking. In that sense, the brain is malleable. It can change and it can heal itself.

You can train your brain to adopt a positive outlook or positivity bias through your thoughts. This can be done through the process of daily affirmations and regular visualisation. It is important to challenge negative thinking with more realistic opposition, in doing so your new and more optimistic thoughts will replace your old ways of thinking.

Both regular physical exercise and on-going learning can help harness the brain's ability to rewire. It can help protect against organic illness and also protect mental wellbeing too. We must also safeguard our mind from negative discourse that may also cause changes to brain chemistry. You will know the effects that music has on your brain, the choices you make can directly impact on your emotions, but also the lyrics can also change your neurochemistry too. If you constantly watch the news, focusing on impending economical doom, then there will be little option to feel positive. You can make direct changes to your lifestyle by choosing to listen to life and positivity affirming messages, ensuring that your brain is exercised, and that which is ingrained in it is good.

Here are a few tips to support your new role as neuroplastician:

- Be mindful of what you listen to, whether this is music or TV
- Try to avoid reading negative press
- Focus on daily positive affirmations
- Visualise
- Choose to live a positive lifestyle

- Exercise your brain through ongoing learning

Research into the field of epigenetics has shown that our thoughts, and therefore our speech, have an influence over our physical health. We can actually think ourselves sick. The mind is a positive tool. We are only beginning to grasp its full potential.

Coach's Top Tips:

Remember your motivating factors for achieving. When you step out to achieve a goal, know that there is a price to pay for the reward. Delaying immediate gratification can lead to long term celebration of success. Are you prepared to work hard now, to win later?

Follow the Pareto Principle. Remember 80% of success comes from 20% of your work. Reflect on the work that brings the greatest rewards and build on that.

The *Be Your Own Coach: Your Pocket Guide* is filled with doses of inspiring messages from the world of positive psychology. I am hoping that you can take hold and make use of this little charm and begin to make new and lasting changes in your life. You are just one step away from achieving your goals. Take that step now.

29147849R00061

Printed in Great Britain
by Amazon